DARE TO DECLARE

Greeting the Day with Intention

MARIA R. MALEC

WestBow Press books may be ordered through booksellers or by contacting:

WestBow Press
A Division of Thomas Nelson & Zondervan
1663 Liberty Drive
Bloomington, IN 47403
www.westbowpress.com
1 (866) 928-1240

Interior Image Credit: https://support.canva.com/legal/licensing/free-elements/

Back Cover Photo Credit: Sabrina Hendley

ISBN: 978-1-9736-9820-3 (sc)
ISBN: 978-1-9736-9821-0 (e)

Library of Congress Control Number: 2020913150

Print information available on the last page.

WestBow Press rev. date: 9/4/2020

WestBow
P R E S S®
A DIVISION OF THOMAS NELSON
& ZONDERVAN

"Maria is so in touch with her powerful feminine instinct. She's naturally gifted at determining what natural healing practices serve her clients best. It's amazing how she helped me choose the right essential oil and supplements to relax, focus, heal and feel empowered."

Darieth Chisolm, Miromar Lakes FL
Emmy Award Winning TV Host, Life & Business coach
50shadesofsilence.com

"Maria's passion, knowledge and expertise for comprehensive wellness is pretty spectacular. As a wife, a mother and a business owner, she has taken her vast experience in life and in business and created an oasis that brings peace and wellness to our lives. She has done this by ridding her home and her mind from negative, toxic elements and she has produced products and training that show us how to do the same. Even my kids have been massively impacted by her. If you are at a stage of your life where you want to achieve both peace and vitality, Maria is your girl!"

Linda Potgieter, South Africa
Woman, Wife, Mom
Founder, LindaPaige.com

"Like Tiger Woods is good at golf- Maria Malec is good at healthy living and coaching. She incorporates a life time of learning and synthesizes many modalities and can save you so many years. I highly recommend her!!"

Hunter Boon, Napa Valley, CA
Entrepreneur, Founder, Project248.com, Partner, Consecrationwine.com

"Maria has guided me in the right direction with oils and healthy living for the past 17 years since I was pregnant with my first child. She has offered suggestions of what essential oils to use for a healthy pregnancy, then for my babies, my self, my home and even my pets! We are grateful to her for sharing her passion with us. She has impacted our lives greatly."

Susan Chegar, Raleigh, NC
Mom, Wife, Artist

"Maria has a gift at helping people tap into your deepest emotions and turn your patterns into a progressive direction to being your highest best self. The aromatic oils application with deep breathing is a gift to achieving a state of bliss. I highly recommend her to EVERYONE."

Valerie, Tarpon Springs, FL
Wife & mom

Dedicated to

Who I AM today

Gratitude for
EVERYONE & EVERYTHING
You are all My teachers.
Most especially, my Divinely chosen Mom & Dad, Joseph and Madeline Longo
My husband, Steve, and children Stephen, Josef, Madelin, Caleb and Jakob
for affording me the freedom to be who I AM
My trusted guides and mentors
Dexter Godbey, Jerry Hurley, Michael Jeffres & Hunter Boon

*"If you can overcome yourself at the beginning of the day,
the rest of the day will be easy."*
Dr. Gregg Braden

I GREET TODAY...

as a CONDUIT of inspiration from my Creator. This book radiates affection from the One that gives us breath and life.

Starting the day filled with intention creates a ripple of goodness and paves the way for treasures to unfold.

Do you consider yourself thriving, maintaining, just getting by or surviving?

The fact that you are here is very proof that your life has meaning. Wouldn't you agree? Otherwise, why are you here?

If you believe that your words have tremendous power, then you will really enjoy this read for its ability to stir up emotion and to significantly contribute to your health and wellness. It will unleash your entire world. What's going to happen as you continue to use this book is that you will be able to navigate through life's many paths and passages with greater ease.

We have been conditioned to view the world through our brains. Most of us think that the brain drives the heart. Yet, it is only through harmonizing the heart and the brain that we are complete and can experience the capability to process things faster without the logic, fear and doubts of the brain alone. This book serves to help you reestablish the connection between heart and brain and re-root you to your original design.

How to use this book...any way you please! Seriously. Only you know how you feel and the way you like to handle things best. However, for those of you who like to mix things up, I will offer some suggestions for you to make the most of these declarations.

Let's begin by exploring what is needed for the heart and brain to affectively employ daily declarations. With the proper tools and consistent, simple practices heart/brain coherence can positively affect your physical well-being. The process that you learn here will set you up for lifelong wellness. You no longer need to be a prisoner of your mind and can effectively find freedom and relief, a sense of safety, increased confidence and a renewed hope for your future. How great is that?

What I believe is key to learning new methods is having a basic understanding of how things work. Thoughts are the vocabulary of the brain. The brain responds to a **visual** that is associated with an *emotion* and then the *repetition* of both. Emotions are the vocabulary of the body. Feelings are as indispensable to humans as the signals in your car. Turning them off with pharmaceuticals, alcohol, excessive exercise, or other addictions is like driving a car without signals. There is a better way and why this book is in your hands.

What we focus on expands, whether it's good or bad, which is why you need to pay close attention to your thoughts and words. Since your brain works best with pictures, which is why those unsavory emotions are that much more painful, your mind doesn't know if it is observing a situation or if the situation is truly happening. If you are picturing an event repeatedly, your brain and body are responding as if it IS happening now. Your body is creating the chemistry that expresses itself in those persistent emotions. Sadly, these bodily signals are the things that someone who is suffering, is desperate to turn off. Thankfully, it is these emotions that alert you to what needs attention.

Why Declare?

This book brings awareness to the power of the spoken word. Using sound as therapy has a long history. Stress pulls us out of coherence. Sound is a key component to putting us back in tune. An out of tune body expresses itself in a variety of ways like the things we label for sickness. Without expanding on all the science-ey aspects of sound and how it works in healing (that's what Google is for), just consider what better way to affect yourself positively, than with your own voice? Are you marveling, yet, at how easy it is to self-regulate without any external aides? You already have everything you need within you. Your greatest hurdle is to be AWARE of each opportunity to consistently use what you learn.

Why 63 Declarations?

Most people have learned that it takes 21 days to create a new habit. This is partially correct. In 2018, I attended a brain conference in Texas conducted by Neuroscientist, Dr. Caroline Leaf of THINK LEARN SUCCEED. She explained that, "It takes 21 days to build a long-term memory and it takes 63 days to build a new habit. Be wary of anyone who promises a quick fix to a problem-the results will only be temporary."

Despite what you currently believe, the power is within you to shift the way you think and feel. This process is powerful and effective if you incorporate it daily. According to Leaf, "Repetition is necessary for protein synthesis and consolidation of memory." Don't let the simplicity of this law of attention fool you. When properly executed, amazing things happen.

Why use essential oils?

Like sound, essential oils have a long history of use for affecting positive change. One of their most powerful uses is to imprint a new thought process in the brain's emotional storehouse called the limbic system.

Through scientific clinical research, essential oils have been shown to vibrate at a higher electromagnetic frequency than any other substances measured. If you're sick or unwell, your vibrational frequency[1] will be lower.

If you're healthy and well, your vibrational frequency will be higher. In human beings, vibrational frequency can be measured with a biofeedback machine that gives a reading in megahertz (MHz). This is key to know because things like negative thoughts, processed foods, chemicals, pharmaceuticals and toxins in the environment will lower your vibration. Low vibration opens the door to dis-ease. We are very sophisticated electrical machines. A good way to understand this concept is to think of the difference between a charged battery compared to a drained battery and its ability to power optimally.

The most remarkable aspect of using oils during this process is that smell physically connects your feelings and visual to your brain. What this means is that even if you forget how you felt, what you pictured or what you declared during the process, you will continue to reinforce the neuropathway or newly imprinted thought in your brain by repeated inhalation of the oil. This tiny bit of information is incredibly powerful to comprehend and thus utilize for optimal wellness.

Though there are three basic uses of essential oils; smelling, applying topically or taking internally, for purposes of this book, we will be using essential oils through inhalation only. It is one of the easiest and quickest ways to affect your brain, as well as, create an environment within your body that builds, nurtures and supports well-being.

Resource

1. Young, Gary. "Human Electrical Frequencies and Fields." Uploaded by the Nikola Tesla Institute, Scribd. Accessed May 30, 2019

*"A truly 'normal' state of consciousness is one that is free of all
negativity and instead filled with joy and love."*
Dr. David Hawkins

Here are some ways on how to use this book to shift the way your body responds to what you are declaring to it and to the vibrational world. The process will give you the ability to influence change through new lenses where you can create a life, experiencing everyday wellness without turning off your emotions. What you will find is that if you succeed at going the full sixty-three days without skipping a day, you will have created a habit of starting the day in this intentional way. By day sixty-four it will feel unnatural to start the day in any other manner. With diligent self-awareness you can effectively overwrite faulty programming every two and a half months. Can you imagine who you would be in just a year? The potentiality is so exciting to me. You can have a different life. This really works. Be like Nike..."Just do it".

START Here! Read your daily declaration out loud with conviction

1. Read straight through this book daily from Day 1 to Day 63. This is the simplest way to train your brain to greet your day by setting it up in a positive, intentional way. Put this book on your nightstand, in the bathroom, by your sink, next to the coffee maker, in your car or anyplace visible that you will be reminded to read because it is something you do regularly every day. It's important to keep it in the same place to exercise the muscle of repetition and consistency.

2. Choose one declaration that resonates with you. Read that single declaration for the full sixty-three days. Then start over with another for sixty-three days and so on. This book will serve you for years doing it this way. What an awesome investment in yourself! Journaling the experience is highly recommended. You

will marvel at your metamorphosis when read the sixty-three-day chapter of your life.

3. Read the book as a part of your daily contemplative practice. Let the declaration serve as your mantra. Since I like variety in my routine, contemplation/meditation can take place while you are brushing your teeth, sweeping, gardening, walking or biking, washing the dishes, doing laundry, putting away the groceries, mowing the lawn, walking the dog, painting or any activity that you give 100% of your attention to. This is an opportunity to put down the electronics and turn in.

4. Take a declaration or multiple ones and write them on notecards. Place the notecards in places that you will see them during your day. Writing them down increases the effectiveness of the process because you are engaging the sense of touch.

5. Read the book with a group of friends. Choose the same one or individually. Discuss the process with each other. Guide, support and celebrate.

6. The Ultimate experience and my favorite way to Declare the Day

Step 1: Choose a declaration

Step 2: Create a Visual

Use the picture in the book or form one in your mind to envision while you repeat the declaration statement. Only use one statement at a time. You can only focus on one image at a time anyway.

Step 3: Attach Corresponding feeling to visual.

During this step, infuse your image (from the visualization in Step 2) with a good feeling. How does your image bring you joy? Fully FEEL what you see. This is the most important component to this exercise. Memories (pictures/visuals) are always attached to an emotion. As you repeat an affirming statement with a visual that is attached to a positive feeling, you will start to feel the new effects of the reprogramming process. When you give your mind new images to focus on you effectively begin to heal from the damage of a self-sabotaging mindset.

You can only think one thought at a time. If you are consistently putting your attention on self-affirming statements coupled with an enjoyable visual and positive corresponding feeling, you will begin to see your life transform.

Step 4: Inhale an essential oil while declaring the daily intention. Take a few deep breaths inhaling the oil of choice and fully immerse yourself in the feeling and visual.

Step 5: Pull it all together by employing all your senses during the process. **Place your hand over your heart.** Your brain goes to where the touch is and can successfully drop into your heart. Slow down your breathing. Slowing down the breath signals to your body that you are safe.

Next, **cross your legs** because this engages both sides of your brain. In addition to their many functions, each side of the brain manages the opposite side of the body. What science has shown is that when the limbs are crossed, both sides of the brain are activated. With both sides of the brain working concurrently, the brain spheres synchronize, which means you are using whole brain activity.

Finally, **put a smile on your face**. Yes, really! <u>Dr. Isha Gupta</u> a neurologist from IGEA Brain and Spine explains, "a smile spurs a chemical reaction in the brain, releasing certain hormones including dopamine and serotonin." How extraordinary that a mere act of smiling can lift your mood, lower stress, and boost your immune system?

Stay in this place for as long as you need to. Can you understand, now, how setting up your day with a daily declaration can contribute to your overall well-being? Once you consistently integrate any one of the processes above your body and mind will reflect the fruit of its effectiveness through affirmative wellness.

Step 6: ALLOW all to flow like a river.

BONUS: Forgiveness Relief Flow

During Step 5 Go through the following process of liberty through forgiveness.

Declare all out loud. Record on your phone and playback to yourself, if you want to keep your eyes closed. Play soothing music or sounds in nature.

Contemplate on the following:

- I give myself permission to allow myself to be forgiven & to heal

- I surrender fear

- I release judgement

- I forgive myself for self-hatred

- I release myself from the bondage of blame and shame

- I forgive myself for blaming myself for the things I never created

- I love every part of me as I Am

- I love others because I love myself

DISCLAIMER

Let's be real for a minute.......

The information contained in this book is meant for educational and informational purposes only. I am not a doctor. I'm #justamom who really digs sharing my knowledge about living well. Neither do I dispense medical advice on curing nor treating any health ailment or disease nor do I have a degree in health, medicine or nutrition. I only discuss my own experiences and what works for me or my family. If you need medical advice, find a local doctor or nutritionist to provide it for you.

The statements in this book have not been evaluated by the FDA. Information here is not intended to diagnose, cure, treat, or prevent any disease. Readers are advised to do their own research and make decisions in partnership with your healthcare provider. If you are pregnant or nursing or have a medical condition or are taking any medication, please consult your physician. Nothing you read here should be relied upon to determine dietary changes, a medical diagnosis or courses of treatment. The author does not accept responsibility for such use.

Essential oil quality level

Quality counts! Be aware that there are four grades of essential oil quality. Just know that the results you are seeking in this book are from the contribution of the highest quality available. The four grades are as follows: 1. Therapeutic Grade A, safe for internal use and are pure and unadulterated 2. Natural/Food Grade B, natural oils (organic) and certified oils. Can still have chemicals 3. Perfume Grade C, extended or altered, contains chemicals and solvents 4. Floral Waters Grade D, low quality synthetic or nature-identical oils. They go into hair and skin products.

If you are pregnant or nursing, these oils are recommended to avoid: basil, clary sage, fennel, hyssop, nutmeg, rosemary, sage, tansy and tarragon.

Contact me directly, if you need assistance in selecting the highest-grade oil.

I Greet Today . . .
with endless possibilities

Day 2

I Greet Today . . .
with GRACE and Ease

Day 3

I GREET TODAY...
with
JOYFUL
anticipation

Day 4

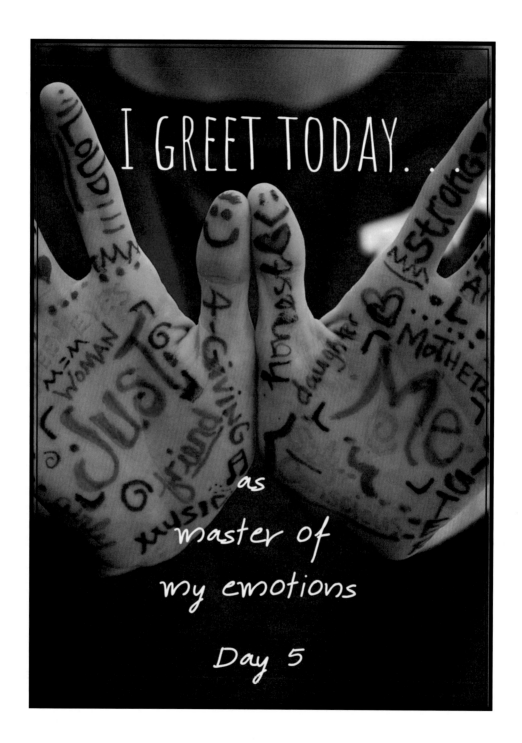

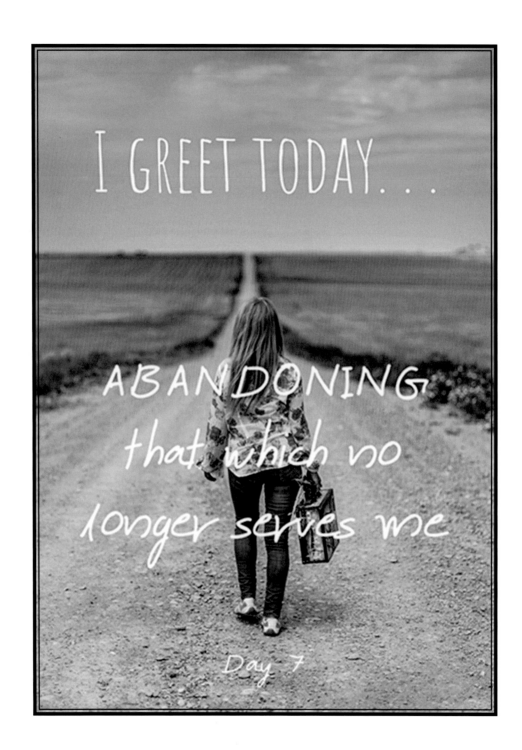

I GREET TODAY...

ABANDONING
that which no
longer serves me

Day 7

I GREET TODAY...

with AWARENESS
of my surroundings

Day 8

I GREET TODAY . . .

with
ACCEPTANCE
of where
I am

Day 9

I GREET TODAY...

at PEACE
about where I'm going

Day 10

I GREET TODAY. . . .

EXPECTING
great things to happen

Day 11

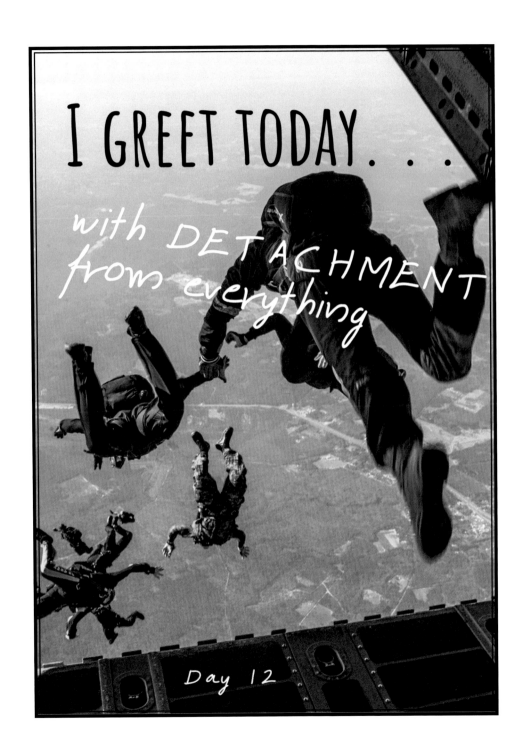

I GREET TODAY . . .

with DETACHMENT from everything

Day 12

23

I GREET TODAY . . . with MINDFUL inner dialogue

Day 13

I GREET TODAY...

with
heart and mind
COHERENCE

Day 14

I GREET TODAY. . .
with the KNOWING
of how to self-align

Day 15

26

I GREET TODAY...

with RELIEF from my distress

Day 16

I GREET TODAY . . .

with

child-like

WONDER

Day 17

I GREET TODAY...

SURRENDERING
the need to control

Day 18

I GREET TODAY...

FEEDING

my body & brain

with living foods

Day 19

I GREET TODAY...

BLESSING every cell in my body with healing light

Day 20

I GREET TODAY. . .

with the
UNDERSTANDING
that my negative experiences
dont define me

Day 21

I GREET TODAY. . .

FORGIVING those who have intentionally or unintentionally hurt me

Day 22

I GREET TODAY. . .

by RELEASING myself
from the bondage of
blame and shame

Day 23

I GREET TODAY...

Being more AWARE of what's worth my energy

Day 24

I GREET TODAY. . .

in the stillness of
REFLECTION

Day 25

I GREET TODAY...

KNOWING that treasures will show up in simple things

Day 26

I GREET TODAY...

CONNECTED to
my true purpose

Day 27

I GREET TODAY...

ATTRACTING success
and abundance with ease

Day 28

I GREET TODAY...

TRUSTING my
inner intelligence
to guide me

Day 29

I GREET TODAY . . .

Learning to LET GO to receive

Day 30

I GREET TODAY....

RECEIVING grace and goodness as the order of my day

Day 31

I GREET TODAY...
by reflecting
PEACE
which comes from
within not from
what others think
of me.

Day 32

I GREET TODAY. . .

OBSERVING
the extraordinary
in the ordinary

Day 33

I GREET TODAY . . . .

CULTIVATING soul-based relationships

Day 34

I GREET TODAY . . .

CHANGING the world through the best of me.

Day 35

46

I GREET TODAY. . .

with the BELIEF in my ability to heal myself

Day 36

I GREET TODAY....

REFUSING the tendency to criticize, condemn or complain

Day 37

I GREET TODAY. . .
UPLIFTING everyone
I meet this day

Day 38

I GREET TODAY . . .

with
ATTENTION
to detail

Day 39

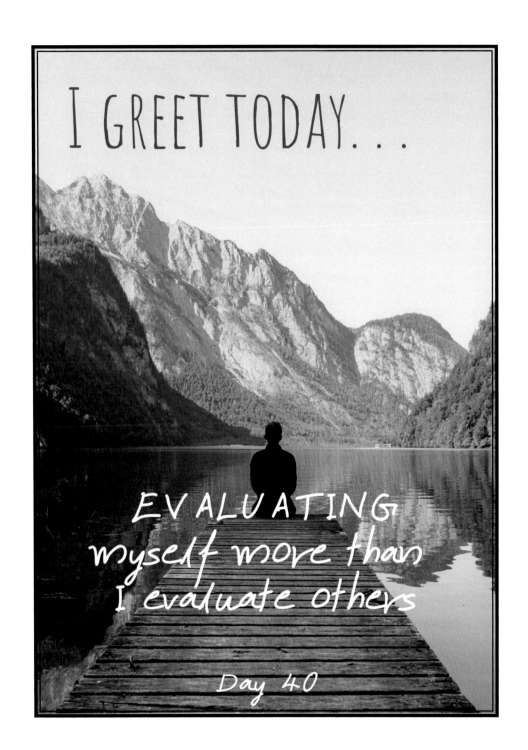

I GREET TODAY....

EVALUATING myself more than I evaluate others

Day 40

I GREET TODAY...

Finding FREEDOM
owning my own choices

Day 41

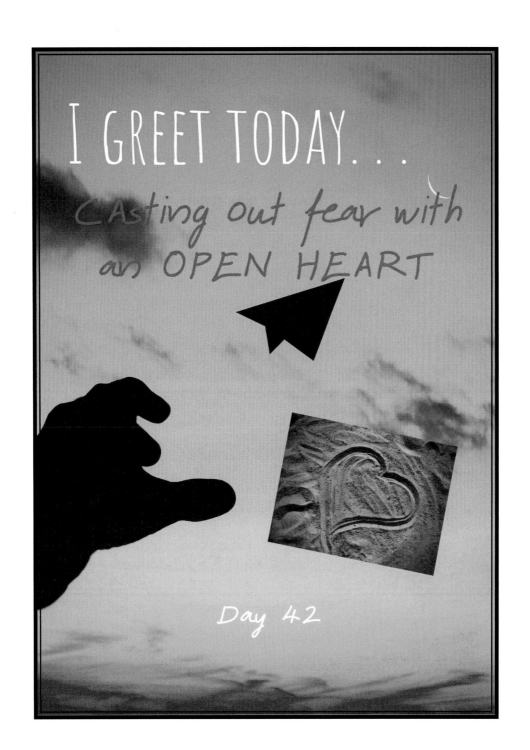

I GREET TODAY. . .

CAsting out fear with an OPEN HEART

Day 42

I GREET TODAY...

ACTIVATING the angelic realm over my loved ones

Day 43

I GREET TODAY.

AFFIRMING that I am safe and all life loves and supports me

Day 44

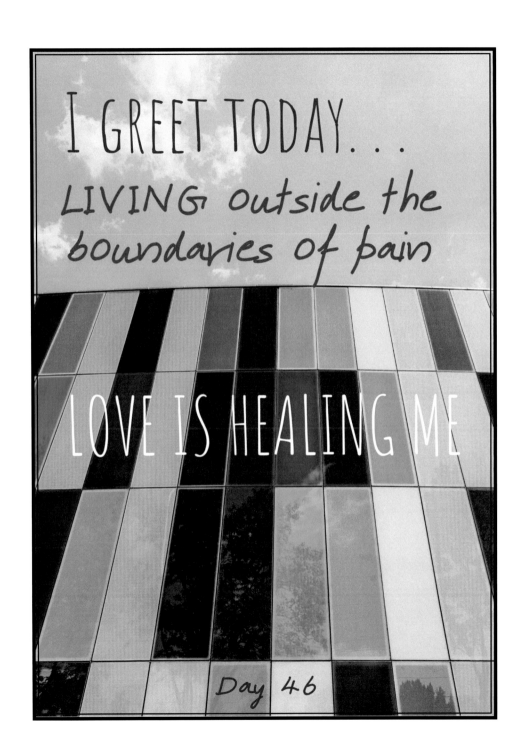

I GREET TODAY...

INTENTIONALLY pursuing
a connection with others

Day 47

I GREET TODAY...

LOVING every part
of myself unconditionally
and Irrevocably

Day 48

I GREET TODAY....

PREPARED to confidently take an unknown path

Day 49

I GREET TODAY...

RADIATING Bliss

Day 50

I GREET TODAY...
Appreciating that I am
WORTHY of every good thing

Day 51

I GREET TODAY...

Being
FAITHFUL
with the little things

Day 52

I GREET TODAY....

HONORING
my spirit within

Day 53

I GREET TODAY...

LIVING
in peace & victory.
completely
FREE

Day 54

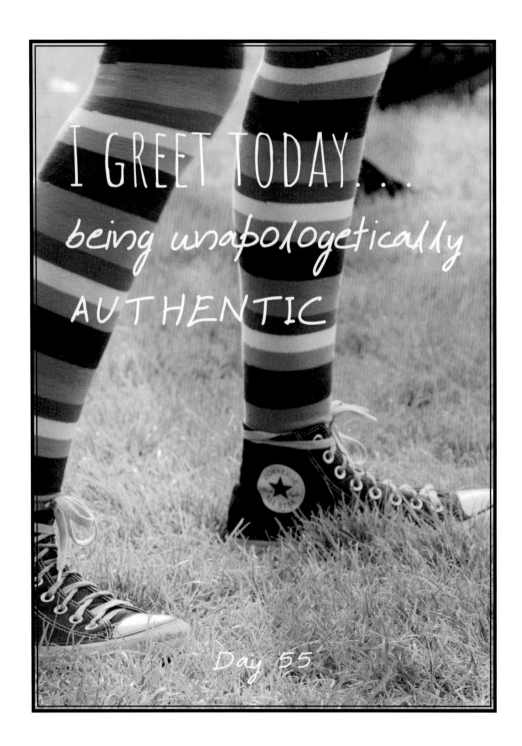

I GREET TODAY...
being unapologetically
AUTHENTIC

Day 55

I GREET TODAY...

FOCUSED ON
impacting lives

Day 56

I GREET TODAY...

RESPECTING
all life as it was
created

Day 57

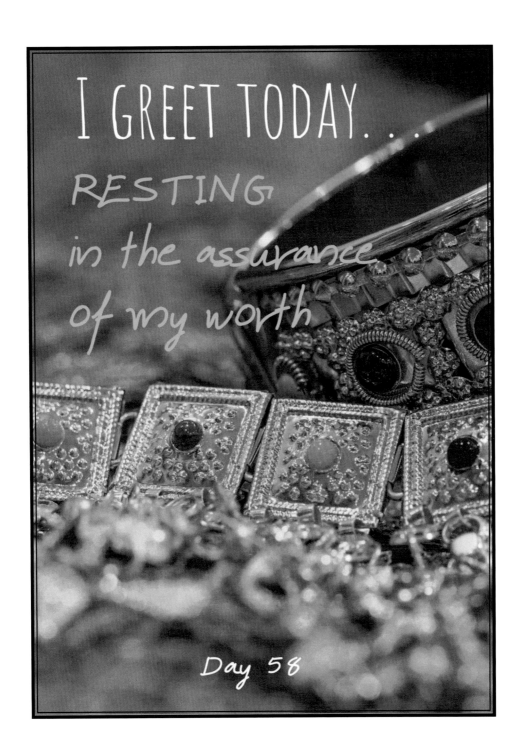

I GREET TODAY...
RESTING
in the assurance
of my worth

Day 58

I GREET TODAY...
BLESSING others with

GRACE

LOVE

MERCY

Day 59

I GREET TODAY....

Using my pain to MOTIVATE me

Day 60

I GREET TODAY . . . . .

being VULNERABLE to become strong

Day 61

I GREET TODAY. . .

CELEBRATING
all the moments

Day 62

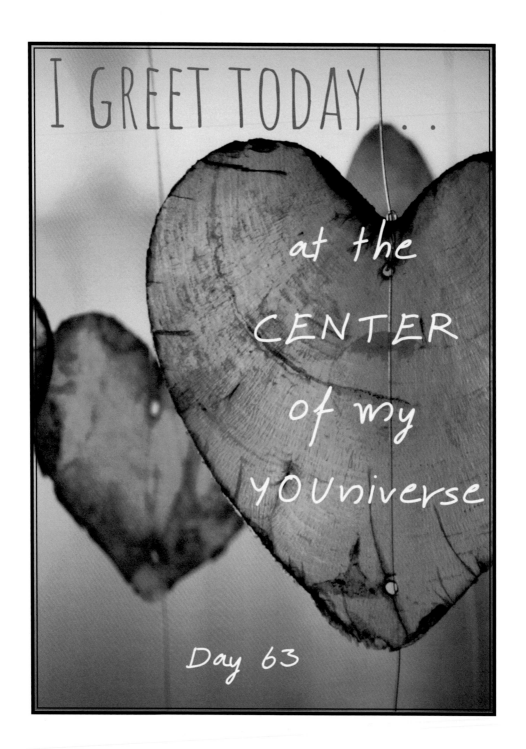

I GREET TODAY . .

at the CENTER of my YOUniverse

Day 63

Notes & Creations

Take your wellness to the next level work with
Maria R. Malec, Your Wellness Guide

90 Day Fresh Start Program: In just 90 days you will confidently learn the 4 Keys of The Self-Care Code to consistently live above the wellness line every day. Her family is living proof that it works. *partial program proceeds to charitable cause

Inquire via email below.

Stay Connected:

Email: aromalivingbydesign@gmail.com

Website: www.aromalivingbydesign.com

Instagram: @mariamalecjustamom

Facebook: @aromalivingbydesign

Essential Oils: https://MariaMalec.marketingscents.com
813-957-0865

 FREE FALL INTERNATIONAL
FOUNDATION, INC.

Fall International Foundation, LLC
501C 3: #82-4924029
Mission: Funding those suffering from emotional, physical and psychological trauma who are seeking restoration and rehabilitation through natural and holistic methods.
"Life is a free fall. We are your safety net."

Printed in the United States
By Bookmasters